Copyright © 2011 the Thinking Tree, LLC
All rights reserved.

Dyslexia Games Series B-Book 7
Friendly Copyright Notice:

ALL DYSLEXIA GAMES, WORKSHEETS, AND MATERIALS MAY <u>NOT</u> BE SHARED, COPIED, EMAILED, OR OTHERWISE DISTRIBUTED TO ANYONE OUTSIDE YOUR HOUSEHOLD OR IMMEDIATE FAMILY (SHARING IS STEALING).

Please refer people interested in Dyslexia Games to our website to purchase their own copy of the materials.

The Thinking Tree LLC • 617 N Swope St. • Greenfield, IN 46140 • info@dyslexiagames.com • +1 317-622-8852

Silly Animal Rhymes

Sweet & Silly Animal Poems, Drawing Games & Spelling Lessons.

By Sarah J. Brown

Parent Teacher Instructions:

Provide the student with a pencil, eraser, a set of sharp colored pencils, and a fine point black pen.

This workbook requires the teacher to spend a few minutes reading with the child. Before your student begins each lesson read the short poems on the page while the child listens. Then read it again and have your student repeat each line back to you. Read the poem a third time together while the child points to each word.

The page of the right is there for the child to add his own words to the poem; he may need help spelling. If he is not ready for creative writing he can fill in the missing word instead. There is a list of words on the first page of the workbook that appear through out the workbook. He can choose from the list of words or come up with his own ideas. You can also have a word hunt, looking for the words on the list.

The empty box is for the child's drawing to go along with his silly poem.

Give the child time to add color to the animals on each page, if he is in the mood to color.

Animals
(Nouns)

turtle	butterfly	beetle
kitten	pig	horse
mouse	goat	dog
lamb	mouse	chicken
puppy	bunny	dolphin
squirrel	duck	bear
snail	ladybug	fish
slug	frog	guinea pig
rooster	bee	seal
rabbit	tiger	donkey
bird	toad	cat

Places & Things
(Nouns)

pond	birdhouse	shoe
ice-cream	seeds	road
tree	garden	jar
string	crust	flower
beans	apple core	dollars
house	coat	ball
zoo	kale	forest
pet shop	pail	sun
house	cage	rays
farm	yard	pets
carrots	branches	umbrella
leaves	yard	neighborhood
	baseball	

Action Words
(Verbs)

found	turn	tie
taste	brush	heard
play	eating	nibble
chase	hid	watch
own	follows	play
climb	remembers	come
catch	climb	sit
build	think	keep
hang	hide	jump
waiting	stay	smile
save	learned	splash
sing	train	

Descriptive Words
(Adjectives)

little	blue	hard
pretty	purple	busy
grey	dozen	big
brown	favorite	silly
good	fun	soft
slimy	friendly	fluffy
fast	special	good

© 2011 all rights reserved. The Thinking Tree, LLC

I found a turtle by the pond and named him Mr. Green.
I let him taste my ice cream cone, and gave him all my beans.

Little kitten, play with me. Here is a catnip mouse.
Little kitten, chase my string all over the house.

Add your own words and picture to make a silly poem.

I found a _____ by the _____
and named him Mr. _____.
I let him taste my _____,
and gave him all my _____.

Little _____, play with me.
Here is a _____.
Little _____, chase my _____
all over the _____.

Mary had a little lamb, I'd like to have one too.
When I grow up I want to own a pet shop, farm or zoo.

Puppy dog, puppy dog, are you lost and alone?
You chased a pretty butterfly, puppy please come home.

Add your own words and picture to make a silly poem.

Mary had a little _____,
I'd like to have one too.
When I grow up I want to own
a _____, _____ or _____.

Puppy dog, puppy dog,
are you _____ and _____?
You chased a pretty _____,
puppy please _____.

Little squirrel, I'm like you, I love to climb the trees.
Little squirrel, be my friend, we'll play with nuts and leaves.

Snails and slugs are grey and brown, sometimes they are green.
Snails and slugs make good pets if you like slimy things.

Add your own words and picture to make a silly poem.

Little _____, I'm like you,
I love to climb the _____.
Little _____, be my friend,
we'll play with _____ and _____.

Snails and _____ are _____ and _____,
sometimes they are _____.
Snails and _____ make good _____
if you like _____ things.

Sometimes I chase the rooster, sometimes he chases me.
But I can never catch him, unless he's fast asleep.

I'd like to catch that rabbit, but he's too fast for me.
So I will build a rabbit house with carrots and green leaves.

Add your own words and picture to make a silly poem.

Sometimes I _____ the _____,
sometimes he _____ me.
But I can never _____ him,
unless he's fast _____.

I'd like to _____ that _____,
but he's too _____ for me.
So I will build a _____ _____
with _____ and _____.

I'm building you a bird house and filling it with seeds.
I'll paint it blue and purple and hang it in a tree.

Butterfly, butterfly, my garden's in bloom
My flowers are waiting, I hope you come soon!

Add your own words and picture to make a silly poem.

I'm building you a _____
and filling it with _____.
I'll paint it _____ and _____
and hang it in a _____.

Butterfly, butterfly,
my _____ ____ _____
My _____ are _____,
I hope you come soon!

Little piggy, here I come with something just for you!
I saved my crusts and apple cores, and carrots from my stew!

Spring is here and birds appear. In every tree they sing.
It's my favorite time of year when winter turns to spring!

Add your own words and picture to make a silly poem.

Little _____, here I come
with something just for you!
I saved my _____ and _____,
and _____ from my stew!

Spring is here and _____ appear.
In every _____ they sing.
It's my favorite time of year
when _____ _____ _____ _____!

I'd like to have a dozen goats, I'd be happy with just one.
I'd teach it tricks, and brush its coat, and take it for a run.

A mouse was in my garden eating beans and kale.
When kitty came to catch him, he hid beneath a pail.

Add your own words and picture to make a silly poem.

I'd like to have a dozen _____,
I'd be happy with just one.
I'd teach it tricks, and _____ its _____,
and take it for a _____

A _____ was in my _____
eating beans and _____.
When _____ came to catch him,
he hid beneath a _____.

I had a baby bunny that did not like his cage.
So I put him in the garden, much to Mom's dismay!

My best friend is a friendly duck. He thinks that I'm his mother!
He follows me around the yard. We have so much fun together.

Add your own words and picture to make a silly poem.

I had a baby _____
   that did not like his cage.
So I put him in the _____,
   much to Mom's dismay!

My best friend is a friendly _____.
   He thinks that I'm his _____!
He follows me around the _____.
   We have so much fun together.

There is a special time of year, but I don't remember when.
The ladybugs sneak in my house. I don't know how they get in!

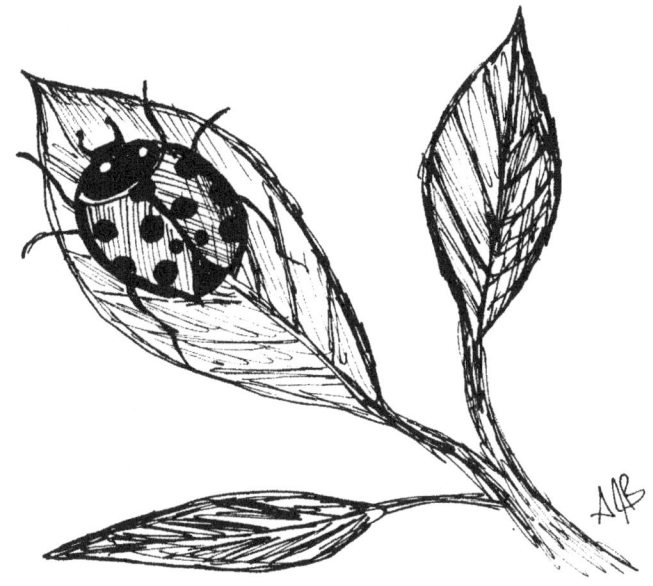

Once I found a tree frog, we both were climbing trees.
I watched him climb the branches and hide among the leaves.

Add your own words and picture to make a silly poem.

There is a special time of year,
but I don't remember when.
The _____ sneak in my _____.
I don't know how they get in!

Once I found a _____ frog,
we both were climbing _____.
I watched him climb the _____
and hide among the _____.

Bees are fun to watch, but stay far from the hive!
I once learned this the hard way, and I'm glad to be alive!

I would like to train a tiger, if I worked at the zoo.

I would teach him to play baseball, and how to tie a shoe.

Add your own words and picture to make a silly poem.

_____ are fun to _____,
but stay far from the _____!
I once learned this the hard way,
and I'm glad to be _____!

I would like to train a _____,

if I worked at the zoo.

I would teach him to play _____,

and how to tie a shoe.

Somewhere along the trail, far from the busy road.
I heard a creature croaking, it must have been a toad.

Little Beetle, there you are! I'd like to put you in a jar.
You can nibble on a flower, while I watch you for an hour.

Add your own words and picture to make a silly poem.

Somewhere along the _____,
 far from the busy _____.
I heard a creature _____,
 it must have been a _____.

Little _____, there you are!
 I'd like to put you in a jar.
You can nibble on a _____,
 while I watch you for an hour.

I'll be riding on a fine horse, when I am twenty-four.
I've saved up fifty dollars, but mom says I'll need lots more.

Dogs are fun to play with. They run and catch the ball.
Dogs will give big kisses and come each time we call.

Add your own words and picture to make a silly poem.

I'll be _____ on a fine _____,
when I am twenty-four.
I've saved up _____ dollars,
but mom says I'll need lots more.

_____ are fun to play with.
They run and catch the _____.
_____ will give big kisses
and come each time we call.

I will sit here in the forest, I will be still for half a day.
The rabbits don't know that I'm here, and I like it this way.

Hens and chicks are silly. Have you ever watched them play?
The chicks are soft and fluffy and the hens have much to say.

Add your own words and picture to make a silly poem.

I will sit here in the _____,
I will be still for half a day.
The _____ don't know that I'm here,
and I like it this way.

Hens and _____ are silly.
Have you ever watched them _____?
The _____ are soft and fluffy
and the hens have much to _____.

Listen to my dolphin sing. Watch her dance and play
When the sun is going down she splashes in its rays.

I'm as happy as a bear cub playing with his mom.
I'm as sleepy as a brown bear, napping all day long.

Add your own words and picture to make a silly poem.

Listen to my _____ sing.
Watch her _____ and play
When the sun is going down
she _____ in its rays.

I'm as happy as a _____
playing with his _____.
I'm as _____ as a brown bear,
_____ all day long.

Goldfish are such lovely pets. They never bark or bite.
They swim and play all through the day, and never pick a fight.

If I were a tree frog I'd climb the highest tree.
I'd sit up there all summer, or until my mom called me.

Add your own words and picture to make a silly poem.

_____ are such lovely pets.
They never bark or bite.
They _____ and play all through the day,
and never pick a fight.

If I were a _____ frog
I'd climb the highest _____.
I'd sit up there all summer, or until my mom called me.

If I had a guinea pig I'd name her "Bonnie Blue".

I'd give her my umbrella and keep her in Dad's shoe.

Two baby seals jump and play, they seem to smile too.

Do you like to watch the seals splashing at the zoo?

Add your own words and picture to make a silly poem.

If I had a guinea pig I'd name her "_____".

I'd give her my _____

and keep her in Dad's _____.

Two baby _____ jump and play,

they seem to _____ too.

Do you like to watch the _____

_____ at the zoo?

My momma had a donkey. That donkey was not good.

My momma had to chase it all through the neighborhood.

Add your own words and picture to make a silly poem.

My momma had a _____.

That _____ was not good.

My momma had to _____ it

all through the neighborhood.

Silly Animal Rhymes

Certificate of Completion

_____

Name & Age

_____

Date of Completion

The Thinking
TREE

_____

Dyslexia Games

_____

Teacher

The Thinking TREE

www.DyslexiaGames.com

Copyright © 2011 the Thinking Tree, LLC
All rights reserved.

Created by: Sarah Janisse Brown

Made in the USA
Middletown, DE
08 March 2020